Good Sons

First published in 2025 by Blue Diode Press
30 Lochend Road
Leith
Edinburgh EH6 8BS
www.bluediode.co.uk

© Tim Craven

The right of Tim Craven to be identified as author of this work has been asserted in accordance with Section 77 of the Copyright, Designs and Patents Act 1988.

ISBN: 978-1-915108-26-5

Typesetting: Rob A. Mackenzie
text in Dante MT Pro

Front cover design: Tim Craven

Diode logo design: Sam and Ian Alexander.

Printed and bound by Imprint Digital, Exeter, UK.
https://digital.imprint.co.uk

Good Sons

Tim Craven

BLUE DIODE PRESS

EDINBURGH

for Amanda

We must risk delight. We can do without pleasure,
but not delight. Not enjoyment. We must have
the stubbornness to accept our gladness in the ruthless
furnace of this world.

– Jack Gilbert

Contents

Neuroanatomy Practical

Smaller than you imagined.
More like your idea of a dog's.
You cup it softly. Your thumb fidgets
over the fissure of a temporal lobe.
You lift it up to the side of your head
and picture your own firing in there –
surging, immortal.
If you were to lob it against the wall,
would it crumble or shatter
or liquefy or combust or bounce
back into your hands, intact?
When she (sixty-six, Caucasian, lymphoma)
donated it to science, was this the promised
afterlife? You consider biting into it
as you would a peach – and, were it not
for bleach-like stench of toxic preservative,
you might.
In ten years' time you will think
what a privilege it was to hold that brain,
brim-filled with tomato soup recipes and original sin
and the smells of late summer and oboe lessons
and self-taught Italian and the night sky:
The Plough, The Great Bear, The Big Dipper.

Bone

My job is to pick; I am a picker.
I harvest stock from the shelves
like ears of corn and pass it
to the ringer at the register
who compiles the orders
and onwards to the amender
who checks the consignment
against the warehouse manifest.
I staple a receipt to the pick-sheet
so it can be removed
by a dispatcher down the line.

A knot of days becomes a week;
weeks pile up like shed skins.

In the beautiful bite of coolness
at 5.30 am, before the sun hits its stride,
before the streets teem, a partial moon
hangs like a half-eaten egg in sky
the pink of a healing wound.
Change feels graspable.
I walk to my shift, my back
worked stiff from yesterday's;
the only remedy is more work.
I pick. I pass. Repeat. Careful
not to suggest improvements.
Bone: the toil has reached the bone.

Good Sons

When we're all together like this
we're full of shit,

trotting out stories that've been told
and retold till they're bent out of shape.

But we pass the wine,
we dish the potatoes,

we nod at the flashbacks
as though it really happened that way.

It takes about a decade
for the human skeleton to dissolve

and replace itself, and every three months
our ten pints of blood

are removed and restocked,
drop by drop.

As the sun fades outside,
the conversation turns

to how he worked his hands raw
to give us a better life

and then he complains for the rest of the night
that we have it too easy.

Were it not for the lens of the eye
and a few other lingering foetal cells

we'd be entirely new people by now.

Fallout

There's a heavily weighted question woven
into the algorithm of the online dating
compatibility questionnaire that imploded
the distance between us. The one about
whether nuclear war would be interesting.
I guess we both answered 'strongly agree' –
bored out of our skulls, slumped on our sofas,
dreaming of watching the fallout unfold
with someone new and beautiful as we
reload fistfuls of popcorn into our mouths, aghast.

Sonnet

This reward is just micro-moles
of dopamine dripping off
the midbrain floor; axon tentacles
crisscrossing the hemisphere-halves;
the caudate nucleus lit up like Reno.
The cut brakes of obsession from 5-HT
siphoned off in the night and runaway hope
spat loose from the amygdala, beating heart
and quickness of breath
just sympathetic circuitry.
I have the science
but the scent
of your apricot shampoo
is inexplicable, inescapable.

The Year of Mania

It was exquisite

        I'd defeated time

A year of
pure voltage

        drinking on the front porch till three a.m.
    eight mile run at six
        at my desk for nine

    I listened exclusively to Sam Cooke on repeat

Never in my life had I said   yes   so often

   Couldn't wait to rise from my bed each morning
         until I stopped going to bed at all

    Afternoons   I soared up to the roof
        to the bleach-clean sky
   started chain-smoking cigarettes

I must have fallen in love a dozen times that summer
        each more crushing than the last

   I cupped my hands   dipped them into the moonlight
        retrieved flashes of silver

    The future stretched into forever
        the past forgiven

   Nothing needed to get done   Everything needed to get done

   I could feel my eyeballs glisten

Moby Dick

We sail, Ishmael & I, for the Sandwich Isles
at sunrise; two privateers with nothing left
to lose, a last night to tarnish, to wish & counter-
wish, to rap our knuckles upon the bar
for a break. But even with a duffel-bag packed tight
with juju & a bandoleer of lucky bones & dead certs,
there's no chance we'll salvage ourselves
from a life adrift at sea.

I reinspect the ticket but it never shows a win,
two-to-one odds-on favourite, Moby Dick,
falling at the first, chasing loss with loss
like a sermon aboard the Pequod.
The brutal rhythms of hooves through turf
& whitecaps slapping the hull
thunder in my head.

Please, just one more reach towards the blessed
& I'll vow to turn blind-eyed
from the rounds of pitch-and-toss & mail home
every meagre pay-packet weighed piecemeal
against the harvest of boiled blubber & ambergris.

Anne Sexton's Thymus

The brain's greatest deceit
was to convince us that melancholy
is an affliction of the heart –
how it punches its way out
past the portcullis of ribs,
how it hangs
like a flower with a broken stem.

And all the emotions of Ancient Greece
were said to have originated
in the dull smoke of the thymus,
sweetbread lodged behind the breastplate.
Translated as rage, life-force, depth –
vestigial emotion.

But it was her brain that gave way
to the dysthymic low
that floated through those bad-souled
Bostonian afternoons,
leading her out to the garage dressed
in her best fur, to her rose-red
Mercury Cougar, its engine ticking over.

Sabbath

O Lord, your repeated motifs break like waves
across these bleakest hours: my shower curtain,
for instance, is printed with palm trees
huddled around yellow mounds of heaped sand

and yet their extravagant samenesses,
their whispers of paradise,
leave me tarnished; pound-shop provenance
evidence of just how far I haven't come.

Standing against the tropical backdrop,
water so crystal you can see the tub, it's clear:
I have been a poor believer, a self-serving believer,
no believer at all. I've burnt through my faith.

The hot rainfall cleans but does not cleanse.
A sea breeze sweeps in,
disturbing the fronds, thick with greenness,
rustling the folds in the plastic curtain.

But under the great height of Sunday night's ceiling
the wind utters nothing intelligible. The stars
contain no magic. Even breathing
requires a great performance.

A gin-stained afternoon still lingers in the veins
of the evening, finely balanced between enough
and excess, loved and unlovable.
I weigh myself against the weekend's damages.

My shadow turns to birds which scatter heavy
into the night.

Spider Hands

Rare and degenerative, the condition arrived
without warning: a Tarantula for an index finger,
its swollen mocha abdomen fused to the knuckle
as though the lines embossed across my palm
were the net of its silk-spun web.
Then a Huntsman where I'd last seen
my right thumb. Doctors counted the eyes,
plucked legs for biopsies;
an experimental ointment was prescribed.
I made do with my hands stuffed in my pockets,
opening jars in an elbow's crook.
I almost forgot my plight until two small Sheet Weavers
busied themselves replacing my pinkies.
Then the Trapdoor, the Wolf, the Brown Recluse.

Why me? Why not the neighbour's son?
I'd chop off my arms were I able to grip
the necessary instrument.
My only solace comes at night
when the inquisitive pointed fingers
of children are tucked up in bed.
I drink whisky and ginger through a straw
and telephone a friend whose own suffering
makes me feel as though I've won a prize.
She has experts stumped: an inoperable alligator
is wrapped around her intestines and any day now
its merciless jaws will snap shut for good.

Flounder

One way I used to meet the rent
was to scoop flounder out of a great
fibreglass tank. Flat beasts
without the tasteful symmetry
of the dorso-ventrally pancaked stingray,
the flounder were caught sideways
in the machinery of evolution:
one eye creeping awfully
around the corner of its face.
I gripped the fanned quarter-moon
of its tail and, with the action
of a backhand smash,
struck its head across
the workbench so its body spasmed
into the curl of the letter C
as though trying to form a final word.

The calmest part: the scalpel,
its medical-grade sharpness
running down the length of the back,
and watching the watery meat separate
under its own tension as the smell
of the wild cold poured from the wound.
I snipped each translucent vertebra,
bent them back, and unpicked
the connective tissue with tweezers.

The adaptive capacity to survive
in freshwater or ocean, I was told,
held the key to human life.
But I was only there for the pension
and the free coffee, harvesting data
from glass electrodes, their points so sharp
they slipped invisibly into spines.

With alpha-waves lapping green
over the oscilloscope, in order
not to sacrifice everything,
I took the fillets off the bone
thinking of batter, of fragrant steam.

Nyuto Onsen
[February 2020]

Said to have been discovered
by a dance of cranes healing themselves
in the hot spring's shallows –
into the embrace
of the ancient warmth we sank,
gently at first and then completely,
into water soft and opaque
as bone marrow soup,
rich and mirrorless, summoned
from somewhere deep and furious,
pooling in a simple forest clearing.
It was the season Akita's sweet cabbage
is harvested from beneath the snow –
February, the last days of winter,
shortly before the year broke apart
on the rocks. We'd later learn the death toll
was already on an uptick
but we were warm in our ignorance,
submerged in the rotenburo,
burrowing our feet into a bed
of forgiving round pebbles,
counting bubbles of sulphur.
A moment suspended in rising vapour,
the calm occasionally broken
by the groan and splash of ice
breaking loose from the ryokan roof
and melting by the time the ripples cleared.
Our buoyancy shifted with each cycle of breath,
as we repositioned our spines against
the worn boulders outlining the bath.
Never had we felt so still, slow, naked.
For a blissful afternoon we forgot
how quietly our lives were shaking out.

Chamonix

The train to Chamonix runs on narrow-gauge
to jink around the slopes of Mont Blanc,
but I missed the last departure after weeks
of wait, arrive, climb aboard, stow the luggage,
lug the baggage, scratch, search for a bed, forage
and blind drunkenness. I lay on the platform,
traced the thin rails up the slope: they looped
then drove beneath a canopy of larch,
returned at the edge of an ice-white glacier,
before the peak was decapitated by a teetering
stack of lenticular clouds like badly piled dinner
plates that might have held *blanquette de veau*.
A soldier spoke to the limits
of my French. He took a cheese sandwich
from wax-paper and tore me half. I boiled water
for coffee on my camp stove until the stationmaster
chased us out. We slept nearby on benches
like casualties awaiting extraction.
I woke to the vehemence of a cloudless sky
with the taste of gruyère repeating
on my breath. The soldier was gone
with my stove and sunglasses. The small red train
strained its way up the one-in-five gradient.
I found the sunglasses in my jacket pocket.

Magic Hour

The sun sits low before setting,
twelve degrees of altitude
for twelve minutes;
blues skip off the heavens;
only indirect light,
that soft marmalade light,
seeps through. Shadows
are less dark;
highlights less impressed.

Magic hour, in this town,
lasts just long enough
to shake the orange dust
from your overalls and punch out.

We drive home together,
our separate ways,
sacrificed to the superorganism.

We'll be back late
enlivened
because we've slowed
to inspect a crumpled tragedy
on the opposite carriageway.

A saffron tunic thrown
over the afternoon, diffuse
at the edges: a belt neither city
nor night. Winter rumbles
in the distance, the dark days
approach with the surrendered
optimism of a borstal.

The sky is a great burnt lake –
any moment a mermaid
might break the skin before disappearing
back below the surface.

The Cosmos Wants to Know Itself

I wish I knew the names of constellations
that order those specks of light into the Greek
and Roman gods. I wish you were next
to me, impressed by me, my knowledge. Facts
that don't impress are useless facts. I think
about the purpose of us. I think about
forever. Space expanding, a balloon
without a bursting point. My mind demands
an end. I read about the multiverse,
an infinite and endless range of all
the variations of the universe.
A different world for every choice we make,
divergent lives that scatter on the wind.
I dream of worlds identical but then
entirely different. A world without
our donuts, or elephants, or music.
A world in which you're sat right here beside
my bed of grass, discussing stars. I think
about another me, somewhere, up there,
a better one. How gravity and quarks
and neutrons stop him promising the world
to anyone who'll listen.

Brooklyn _ NY

It's as though we're in a movie
from a top floor off Atlantic Ave

gazing down on more
interesting versions of ourselves

waking to the wide-open
spaces of morning

cop cars speeding like hearts

the city singing to its birds

beyond the serrated-edge
of the skyline
pearl-white clouds

locals catching sunlight
in their hands as though it were rain

this is what life could have been

Bodies

In a mass grave in the Atacama,
bodies, waiting to be reclaimed,
or not, parch in salt-crusted soil.
Above them, on a hill, an observatory
watches a star collapse, its fury serene,
spewing out billions of borrowed atoms
imprinted with the message
that night offers more truth
because if all light is old light,
there can be no present in which to live.
Pluto looks on, ex-planet, gate-keeper
of hell; history will salvage his
crumbling body just as it recalls
us all.

Holes

I can no longer bathe without sinking
like some drowned shopping basket or decayed
tin can buried at sea.
The wind is no comfort, blowing through me
as though I were an open door or dark
matter, its very existence unknown.

Three straight tubes of space the width of drainpipes
have burrowed through my chest from front to back.
No blood, no lymph or fat, just ghostly voids.
Absence. And so I wait for an outcome.
I wait for the holes to backfill and heal
or for my body to collapse under
its own weight; demolished to make more room.

The Art of Freediving

Breathe-up: fill your chest deep
from your stomach, saturate your throat.
Pack down the invisible, the unviable,
until your blood glows rich and velvet.
Exhale slowly, slowly. Repeat.

Dive darker and smaller, until your heart
at its least ravenous. Ignore your limbs forever
as though they belong elsewhere; the ballast-belt
will drag you under. Fall without flinching
farther into the cool blue, the sun will dim:
turquois then purple to faint flint grey.
Let the weight of water make fists of your lungs.
Stripped of all panic, attend to the silence.

Diagnosis

Beyond the locked double doors
and bored receptionist slyly checking her texts,
I sit facing the psychologist:
two chess players in the park.

A one o'clock appointment,
her questions ripe with the perfume
of a cheese and onion sandwich
that echoes on her breath.

She performs her set-procedures,
jotting down scores, timings, observations,
to place my competencies on a bell-shaped curve
of age-adjusted averages.

Roughly the same age as me
but more accustomed to analysing children.
She gently checks I know right from left,
that I can confidently catch a ball.

As I stumble over the pronunciation
of a list of neologisms
that look like words but aren't,
I am armourless.

I've made it this far without a diagnosis
to excuse the tender embarrassments –
misspelt sentences, botched correspondence,
so much distance.

A nexus of coping strategies, she calls me.
Keep doing what you've been doing,
she says. Slant wiring, she says.
But with my vulnerability confirmed

I can't help but obsess
over a certain wretched teacher
who called me an idiot,
writing me off.

I walk back past the receptionist
into the unaltered outside world
like I'm wading through water
right up to my mouth.

Dead Arm Sonnet

Dead of night. Waking to a limb killed
by your own awkward heft
cutting the supply lines.
The breathless panic of discovery.
You try to slap out the absence
in your lifeless wrist with the motion
of an addict. The slumbering world is oblivious
to the retreating borders of your body.
You keep rubbing, expecting
the pins and needles, the heat, the ascension –
the way you've always been revived.
But what if feeling doesn't return?
What if night spreads into your chest?

Sedatephobia

I grew up in a house on a river,
the water breathing over the rocks,
never leaving me alone with myself,

before moving to within earshot of the sea.
The trawlers would return
to shore in the small hours –

the comfort of whistling
pneumatics unloading the catch,
the radio relaying the forecast.

Now I back onto train tracks
where horn blasts Doppler-shift
in and out of the night.

Self-diagnosed; I can't bear the slow silence
of my thoughts. All day the TV offers

white noise and all night I pray
for the commotion of cats
fighting in the street below,

to block out whatever it is
I can't seem to live with.

Obsessive Morning Sky

Rise as one, red clouds.
Squint clean into the early dawn
and glean what you can.
The celestial swept up
  like post-party debris.
Roads glisten with brittle frost
under the moon's bruised face
and a wash of starfields,
shifting smoke of the unknowable,
dense drifts of the white-hot.
A cipher in Technicolor,
the colour of collapse.
Start at the bottom and fade to blue –
the sun hauled up by pulleys.
A world of roofless people
fading to white.

On Happiness

You sit as still as a paperweight
so it won't get spooked;
one misplaced regret
will send it skittering back
into the croon of the wind.

Maybe coaxed from the edge
of the backwoods by warm
porridge and promises;
maybe delivered by prayer –
it vibrates as fragile as the bones
of a hummingbird's inner ear.

One unwelcome memory
or a single stray atom
could break the spell.
To touch the devastating
thinness of its skin would create
a tiny black hole.

So seldom does this book
fall open at these pages.

Feedback

with the need to destroy
something perfect
I abused your sunburst body

thrashed out the only
three chords I knew
smashed you to the floor

for that authentic
dead man's wheeze
we heard on the 45s

your bowed neck
chipped face
warped belly

that homemade fuzz
formed from the speaker cone's
throat sliced up with a razor

impaled with knitting needles
to achieve the victor's howl
lying down inside

the inrushing tide
of overdriven tubes
to better hear your whine

Near Misses

When I mistook picnic for panic
it ruined my afternoon,

on tender hooks, pondering what wrongs
weight to extract their revenge.

I'm always the escape goat or damp squid
wondering off the beat and path.

It won't phrase me
because for all intensive purposes

I'm taken for granite,
a statue of limitations,

as lonesome as a big blue wail
despite your best witches.

Can you explain my floors
using only lame man's terms?

I'm biting my time –
it's doggie-dog out there.

Kintsugi

I thought about a man I know – the worst type of man –
who will willingly list his flaws and faults with pinpoint insight
yet make no attempt to fix a goddamn thing, 'You'll have to excuse me,
I've always had a short temper,' he'll say, or 'I'm just being honest.'
There's something religious about it, the inconsequential confession –
as though by announcing his corrupt traits, releasing them like a
                                                              piteousness
of doves into the cool morning sky, he is absolved, he is delivered,
nothing new or beautiful reconstituted from the wreckage.
All art emerges from damage. All art is a celebration.

Garbage

after A. R. Ammons

Smash this poem (because this is a poem)
then smash all the poems to pieces,

every effort at verse: the sonnets and sestinas,
the ones in leatherbound books, the ones in caves,

those vital ones hastily scribbled on napkins;
without death there is no wish;

uncouple couplets with a crowbar,
pry off every comma, line-break

after line-break, break them:
know that this is not cruel or ruthless, this is nature,

so wrench out those words, the redundant:
ideas are things are ideas:

fell them, level the forest to the ground;
we'll be able to see further: stamp down on them,

break those feet: words to syllables to grunts
to binary bleeps to silence: dismantle them all,

smelt down the scaffolding: there'll be no half-baked
renovations this time – demolition

down to the roots: new poems must be built,
this is no time for sentimentality:

with your pitchfork handles smash this/these poem(s):
marbles to sand to paste to jam to soup

to consommé to water and oil:
we have exceeded the use by date:

mulch it down to the black and white,
the noise and silence, of every poem:

all the fertility and futility
is right here in this mess: the celestial,

the microscopic, everything breaks down
into this homogenous mess: this fourth-hand copy

of this second-rate poem with its handwritten notes
in HB pencil– the least significant passages underlined:

rub them out, kill them dead: with the freedom to fall
flat on your face at least you're moving forwards:

watch the clock, each second moves away from all
beginnings towards all ends:

so, toss them at the walls, those lovingly
crafted gifts; they are junk now:

throw in a fist and rip out the heart of each one:
I'll no longer recognise this as a poem:

self-conscious, self-referential, self, self, self.
Remember to sweep up the mess; collect it

in a bucket: decant out the black and the white –
we need them both – vacuum filter

each to its purest form – too pure
for all but the hardcore:

reclaim it all: compose compost; it's energy;
it can never be destroyed: the essence of it all:

all poems are love poems, is what we'll say we said,
when the necrosis is over:

they said nothing we can't take back: take them,
spit in your hands, rub them in dust,

fashion a tongue, breath in its mouth,
grow a new language, one better capable,

and more beautiful: a language
that can describe the day our children

begin their decay – we'll need a new language
on that day: reconstruct piece by piece:

document the world from scratch:
fewer sounds to pass up big ideas:

make them as evocative as smells:
as sleek as a new simile: like the best new tools –

hammers of the self, chisels of doubt,

saws to cut the horizon in half –
we shouldn't blame the old tools,

and we don't, but that's no excuse:
an endless stream of endings; this is eternity.

When The Moon Is Out in the Daytime

I was born at six in the morning so I've known more days
than nights. They're piled up behind me like rusting
Transit vans fit for the crusher; to embrace the absence
out of them, to make more room for the days to come.

Fact: if all the empty space between our electrons
and protons were squeezed out, you and I would fit
in this bucket.

You look injured, Moon; a third empty, and two-thirds full
of bright white snake oil. Is that why you're up
in the corner of the afternoon, too broken to rest?

Your nightshift starts in a few; rocking the oceans to and fro.
I've got plans for tonight: I'll drive into its blankness
and just maybe it'll be a classic. A night as perfect
as a racehorse or a fresh layer of frost.

When the day has finally talked itself out, we'll co-create
a romance. Your bloodglow a searchlight; me revving
the engine. The radio'll be playing and it'll go like this:

Three Journeys to Harris

I

Calmac's winter timetable
has taken effect.

Weather permitting, the ferry arrives
in the mouth of the harbour

once a day, unloads, loads, ploughs
its way back into open water.

The steeply pitched roof of the stillhouse
flanked by its smaller replicas –

bottling plant and warehouse number one –
dominate the bay's countenance:

whitewashed and angular,
more kirk than factory,

as though a sermon sits
permanently on the lips of the dock.

*

The Isle
of Harris.

The Romans called it *Adru*:
thick, bulky.

The Norse called it *Hærri*:
higher.

*

I drive the Bays, along the Golden Road,
with the hesitation of a novice.

The groundworks cost a small fortune to lay
in the '40s, linking each one-house anchorage.

Cheviots and Blackface sheep,
the imports and the indigenous,

mingle in the road, mixed breeds
dyed and woven into tweed.

The air thick with brine.
The autumn sun has slung itself low

but the island remains as green and slow
as the blood of a sapling.

So full of distance. The land splints
the ocean, the ocean spurs into the land.

*

A fistful of wind
laden with salt and sea-spite

banks off the Clisham,
kisses the old bell of St Clements,

and gusts over soil pocked
with the fallout of a detonated moon.

It rattles its way
over the narrow neck of the isthmus,

where the distillery sits
on land reclaimed from the bay,

only to be caught in the tight grain
of oak staves

like a butterfly – slate, scarlet, cerulean –
pinned to a specimen board.

*

A conflict of perception:
cool, darkly silent warehouse,
but within each cask
an ocean seethes, hot and ruthless;

the wood, a seawall
to barricade in the carnage.

Temperature, pressure, and volume brawl
within a shifting equilibrium:

the surface tension of the fluid
adheres to timber walls;

capillary action searches
for a means of escape.

*

The upturned hull
of a newly commissioned ship

blanketed by Mount Clisham's
799-metre shadow,

half buried in the bay,
stark against the shore;

the seaweed green warehouse
outside the village

is young and unblemished.
Pristine. Inside,

the racked casks sleep
like unexploded bombs.

*

Turmoil lurks beneath the steel rafters
of the store, molecules scattering

with the ferocity of a billiard break:
colliding and re-colliding, ricocheting

at unpredictable slants.
The raw potential of state unspools,
brings forth low groans from the wood,
wide and sonorous as whale song.

Warmth radiates from inside the ribs
of each cask: entropic, exothermic, brazen.

*

Allowed to cool
for the next ten years,

flecks of burnt oak like flakes
of day-old mascara

will flex, float, and drift
in a suspension of total darkness

like earth dumped in a millpond
will settle gently.

*

A place created from a child's drawing:
hills poured upon hills,

so every gap between two mounds
reveals another mound –

imbricated, ever multiplying,
ever decreasing into the distance –

until the whole horizon resembles
scales on a salmon's belly.

*

The morning air is still,
the horizon sharp and immediate

as though the mainland has been lassoed
and hauled a few miles closer.

The light arrives true and unskewed.
I've begun to feel at home.

*

Locals curse the off-islanders
for driving too slowly.

Off-islanders curse the locals
for driving too closely, and lose

every game of chicken,
surrendering the single-track road

two or three
passing places prematurely.

II

My ferry left late tonight;
an irregular load at Lochmaddie this morning

and all day the lost half-hour
couldn't be recovered.

Up on deck the distillery grows.
The waxing gibbous moon beats down

on the shells of abandoned houses,
their roofs long gone.

*

The encroachment of time.
The gift of time.

The slow pollution of time.
The saturation of time.

Time infiltrating like a dream.
A dream of fire.

*

Of all the options – puncheons
and port pipes, quarter casks

and bloodtubs – the alchemy here
is held within hogsheads and sherry butts

nestled upon one another
like a litter of siblings.

＊

For two hours I wait inside the black plank hut,
squint into the horizon for the pair of golden eagles

that nest along the glen. Had I waited three,
they might have revealed themselves.

＊

Crofters are coming and going,
shovelling draff onto their trailers

to feed their herds, the spent husks
piled outside the stillhouse, still steaming

from the hot wash that flushed the sweetness
but left some goodness.

＊

Jagged fractures of granite
pierce the hillside

erupting from the thatch
of moss and chartreuse.

A refusal of scar tissue
to heal completely.

I sit in the evening, a contemplative
celebration of light.

Light that is somehow softer
and sharper than other lights,

the way I'm both less
and more religious

than my ancestors.
Less pressed into tradition.

Triangles form where the hills
meet the sky meets the sea.

Fragile pleasure,
day gently dying in your hands.

The moment,
a sacrifice.

*

Carved into the stone entrance
of Lews Castle, Leverhulme's motto,

Mutare Vel Timere Sperno
(I scorn to change or fear).

But so many here hold down
half-a-dozen jobs

in preparation for the unexpected
they've come to expect.

*

Casks sitting in isolation –
palletised, stacked, abandoned.

Not hibernating but raging;
caged bears wrestling their way out.

Brimful of thousands of tiny tinctures
of extracted island,

localised microclimates impose
their characters.

★

Magic hour. Mountains glow pink
and collapse into a rose-coloured sea.

I'm stood on the barren surface of Jupiter,
unoccupied till the Clearances forced folk

to scratch themselves into this side of the isle.
Harris holds the crown tonight.

★

The story of Neolithic standing stones
repeatedly repurposed:

great rock giants, allegedly once men
petrified for not converting to the new God.

★

Like glacier melt, soft and blank,
the distillery's water source

tumbles down the hill behind the hotel
from a burn, Abhainn Cnoc a 'Charrain,

the name of which only *Hearachs* can pronounce;
a shibboleth of authenticity.

★

Highland cows, mothers and calves,
block the road to Hushinish,

so I wait, helpless in my rental,
as they edge themselves past,

unaware of their bulk, heads bowed, horns
inches from the paintwork.

*

Hushinish, house headland in Norse,
white sand beach

and jetty gently slanting to the sea.
This morning I watched from the cliffs

a shepherd and a fisherman clad in oilskins
haul six Cheviots onto a small blue boat.

Bleating clouds of fleece
tied together for a voyage across the bay

to begin their new lives
on the untrodden pastures of Scarp.

The underpowered two-stoke outboard
struggled against the slack water.

*

This island, thick with language,
the roiling daily dialogues

in Scots and *Gàidhlig*
like a kettle coming up to the boil.

*

I'm tucked in a corner of the canteen, dipping hunks
of soft white bread into lamb soup,

watching the populations pass through: birds
on their routes south for the winter.

Spring, I imagine, will arrive next,
the machair in full bloom,

corncrakes crexing, the return
of oystercatchers, lapwings, buntings.

*

The dark arts of maturation:
the spirit smoothing itself out,

cracking its bones, detangling its nets,
knocking off the sharp edges.

The feinty smell of new-make youth –
clear, colourless, astringent –

transformed into stewed fruit and
dark chocolate, heather honey and sunlight.

*

Plump little Buddhas
recline in a darkened room

within their remote island monastery –
its earthen floor, its absence of windows.

They silently chant their mantras,
until, gradually, their introspection

grows smaller, richer,
more like syrup.

*

A collection of small-scale oceans,
sealed bucketfuls of North Atlantic,

the moon's gravity tugs
and releases the reservoirs

within them. And when the force of the tide
causes a weakness in the wood to weep

and drip upon the ground,
it is left alone to clot, to heal, to *sugar up.*

*

The decommissioned lighthouse on Scalpay,
proud like a barber's pole.

Books still on the shelves.
The railings rusted fragile.

Vaporised salt
gusts in off the North Atlantic

to crust
on the murky window panes.

*

Across the bay, at the tip of the horseshoe,
the sun glistens from within the cliffs.

Splintered quartz – repeating glints
pacing the stretched summer days.

The tide, defiant, uncoupled from solar hours,
grasps its share of the light.

Late afternoon, the warmth retreating
beneath the waves.

The scene watches back,
wordless,

patiently waiting us
out.

*

You can barely hear yourself breathe
amid the raging molecular din

of this marketplace, this circus.
Moiety traded for moiety,

one carbon chain cracked loose
to be shackled to another, oils exchanged

for fats, paid for with microscopic flecks
of copper stolen from the still's walls.

*

Some will become vast, fabulous rooms
as grand as Versailles,

while the dregs of others will be swigged back
straight from the bottle like rocket fuel

by someone grieving on a back porch
looking up at a brilliant carpet of stars.

*

The spirit receives a counterintuitive love:
distilled and then permitted to gradually degrade

into something ravaged and worthy;
like a child, it doesn't miss a thing,

picks up the songs sung, jokes retold,
holds all the voices we'll lose

before the first bottling, remembers
each warm winter, Indian summer,

the stretches of dreich days
too common to count.

*

On Sundays the machinery shuts down,
so the highland cows, rain water

dripping off their manes,
provide the island's only commotion

when they shake the spray
from their backs.

The sun-bleached bones of those
who wandered from the herd

punctuate the hillside, exposed
outliers, like parables.

The origin of the word 'carcass'
descends from a lost language,

an etymology
for 'premonition'.

*

I watch one of those meteor showers
that experts claim only occur every century or so.

The night sky perfect. A frost already
begins to settle, glistening white and brittle.

My gaze fixes to a northern heading,
across Ursa Major's spine,

and every few minutes a bright dot
shoots through the darkness

towards the Earth, towards me,
like a cooling spark

falling
from a blacksmith's lathe.

*

Free to roam the common land, the white ponies
of Luskentyre graze on washed-up seaweed.

A carpet of wildflowers fringes the beach –
butter, lilac, lapis.

When you put your ear to the ground,
against the lush felt of this meadow,

hymns of the past rise from the marrow.
Swimming in the tired light of a fallen sun,

shadows play against rugged outcrops of broken cliff –
errors, erased and reformed.

It is evening. A glittering dusts the hilltops,
a darkness rising like music.

Death grows less dead
and the hills, the waves, the white ponies of Luskentyre

will be here tomorrow,
just where you left them.

III

On Skye, I sit at Uig harbour,
while the weather claims another day of ferries.

The wind thumps the bonnet
as though the car

were inching through an angry crowd.
Blustering, blowing stiff and angular,

the shifting gale bends chimney smoke
into oblivion. Umami, diesel –

my mouth fills with the green flavours
of the ocean.

★

A temperature spike.
A delay in the cut.

Deliberate avoidances of replication;
inconsistencies baked into the process.

Welcome human errors – handmade
mistakes that taste of deviation.

★

The seagrass folds
against an Atlantic breeze.

Machair, rarest of grasslands.
Sand like caster sugar.

Domed lobsterpots slowly corrode,
drowning in the sea air.

Memories returning to dust.
This will be my last trip.

*

I first arrived in the ferocious eye
of Storm Callum and now this is my final visit,

the other side of solstice,
after the long night moon.

Since I was here last, casks one, two and three
have come-of-age, three years and one day.

Three ghosts solidifying
into their mortal forms.

*

The weather has turned bitter
and the peat fires that heat the homes

have filled the town with the smell
of burnt winter.

A wooden washback – new vat from the mainland –
bulges on the pavement.

Its bulk, carved from Oregon pine,
set against a naked sky

like a giant unable to duck beneath
the lintel of the distillery doorframe.

★

Sparsely scattered trees sway
in the face of an onslaught

– a gale breathing in minor keys –
grey and malnourished,

all sinew and wiry strength,
raging against an end

The thaw will lift death from the hills
but this morning a stench of rot

lingers on the tide. To witness
such impermanence demands a solitude.

Across the bay, a postage-stamp-sized
cemetery remains untended, storm-defeated,

sliding down the hillside. Headstones fight
against their own weight, some falling

onto their backs, others, their faces,
as though all the sorrows of the island,

the grief of the morning, have begun
the long journey to the centre of things.

★

Slate grey skies fringed
by the wide sands of Luskentyre beach.

Cheeks tender and ruddy, pricked
by sub-zero cold. Eyes wet from wind.

The seabirds surf the inrushing squall
that shuttles over from St Kilda.

There's a sorrow lodged in the hills
that won't thaw until springtime.

*

Taillights file away from the evening ferry,
a string of illuminated gemstones

poured from the boat's gawp
and dissolved into darkness.

It will rest here tonight
and become my morning ferry;

the crew will sleep in their bunks, packed tight.
Two weeks on, two weeks off.

*

Today the waves are rolling slowly,
resisting the break and crumble into wash.

No roaring battle cries, just the quiet surging
of the ocean's full weight like ripples of molten glass.

For a moment there's a halt to the rhythm
as though the water questions its breath.

Just as the falter threatens to become
a stall, the swell rears up again.

The Art of Returning

It's like you've never been away, so much so,
it's as though you were never here at all.
That, rather than leaving in some absolute way,
you incrementally disappeared,
gradually claiming invisibility
so when the dogs wanted to play,
they were convinced you were hiding somewhere
and tore around the house in search of your scent.
You got talking to a guy at a bar on 6th St
about the art of returning and how you can't judge
the worth of a city in the rain.
When you got back from the bathroom
he'd put all your drinks on his tab.
An app tells you it's raining there now.
But even in the blistering sun –
cracking the flags as grandpops might say –
your place is, well, whatever. You're not a thing
but the shadow of the thing cast upon the wall:
elongated and awkwardly angular.

The Collective Behaviour of Dinosaurs

I remember a BBC2 show I watched as a kid
depicting the assumed behaviours of a pterodactyl colony –
a pack of males furiously biting one another's grey green bodies
until a single beast climbed to the top of the order
and all others knew to offer their absolute devotion.
He alone would father the entire next generation.
Just as today, seven hundred and fifty years on, one in two hundred
men descend from the DNA of Genghis Khan.
The chief of the pterodactyls grew older,
computerised animation rendering him fragile.
A younger, hungrier animal came forth
glistening and taut, unimpeachable confidence,
and fought the reigning king, likely his father, with no
regard for the past. The son snatched the spoils of inheritance.
The father, tired and gravity ravaged, all scar tissue
and sinew, sunk into himself, exiled to old age,
any legacy departed. His bones were picked clean
by species of opportunists. Everywhere I look, men seem
to be taking their cues from the animal kingdom,
carving up the hunt for themselves.

The Domestication of Wolves

Coaxed down from our dens
scattered across the spent hills,
we were given new jobs in telesales,
in vast call centres devoid of windows.

We've chosen wolves deliberately,
they told us during induction week,
so don't dare abandon your wolfish qualities.

They liked our casual good humour and thick skin.
They liked that we were hungry
for their distasteful work – the cold-calling,
the closing, commission-only pay.

They liked amusing themselves at our repeated
social faux pas. They insisted we punch-in
each day, detangled and disinfected, smart
in smoothly groomed uniformity.

They liked that we didn't scare easily
but could easily scare.
Our negotiations were intimidations.

They liked that they'd harnessed
our savagery and unseated us
as apex predators.

But when we turned our eyes upon them,
asked for a fatter bonus, a better basic,
and allowed the silence to grow
into something malignant and excruciating,

they called us pushy and ungrateful,
said we'd misjudged our place,
said we were wrong
to make such ravenous demands.

But we couldn't go back –
overweight and no longer nocturnal,
our mothers wouldn't recognise our scent
and we'd forgotten how to hunt.

Eight Biographies

[BIO. 1]
Originally born in Brooklyn, [TIM] has now been travelling in
Europe for three days. [TIM]'s aura is purple and their Jungian
colour energy is yellow. In a spooky coincidence [TIM]'s third
favourite number is the number three. [TIM] is researching a
novel about the redeeming qualities of narcissism.

[BIO. 2]
Born just outside Moscow to a father and a mother, [TIM] has
toyed with writing under an ethnically-ambiguous pseudonym.
[TIM] is very white. [TIM]'s biggest fears: going blind, dying in a
fire, dying underwater, fading away.

[BIO. 3]
All [TIM]'s tattoos have fangs and all their dreams have
infernos. [TIM] has worked as a knuckle-puller, longshoreman
and cutter in a box mill. On social media, [TIM]'s writing has
been described as important, vital, necessary, essential and
stunning. [TIM]'s writing has been shortlisted, a finalist and a
runner-up, which is to say, a continuing disappointment. [TIM]
was born with all their moons in Aries, which, they've been told,
explains everything.

[BIO. 4]
[TIM] grew up two streets away from you and attended the
rival school. [TIM] enjoys deep conversations about meaningful
things. [TIM] only donates to charities from which they might
someday benefit. [TIM]'s bildungsroman is fuelled on ham
and cheese Findus Crispy Pancakes. [TIM] strives for ultra-
confessionalism.

[BIO. 5]
[TIM] died in a savage battle of Edward Forty Hands. For
many years, [TIM] thought they were a pulsar star – emitting
light, emitting time. [TIM] was best known as an inventor
of motivational maxims, most notably, *If you believe, you can
achieve*, and the ever true, *The only difference between ordinary and
extraordinary is extra.*

[BIO. 6]
Whenever [TIM] daydreamed about death the critics wondered
whether it constituted suicidal ideation. [TIM] regretted the
irreversible damage done by his failures of kindness and his taste
for opium. [TIM] died in a boating accident off the coast of Italy
in 1822. More at [TIM].net because [TIM].com was taken.

[BIO. 7]
Originally from the liquid core of your dreams, [TIM] lives in
Paris, NY. [TIM] founded the online journal, *Permanent Hiatus*
(currently closed for submissions). Once their cat dies, [TIM]
will enjoy the freedom to travel.

[BIO. 8]
Born on the bank of a river, [TIM] has proven themself capable
of retrieving a rubber brick from the bottom of a swimming
pool. When the ocean is perfectly calm and flat [TIM] feels a
deep sense of guilt when breaking its skin.

Wood Cutting

Summertime, sixpence per brick retrieved from the rubble
mound, sixpence per brick cleaned, knocking off clods of
century-old quicklime with a five-pound lump hammer.
Sweating blood under the bleeding sun, and its end meant a
winter trapped as my father's log-chopping lackey.

Saturday afternoons cutting through offcuts of architrave and
railway sleepers from a joinery firm he passed business to. A
plaid padded shirt and patched-up jeans that failed to keep out
the cold.

Death in the air; rotten bark mulch mixed into the woodpile.
Breath clouding out like yellowfoot mushrooms. I held each
misshapen length of lumber tight while he manoeuvred the
violence of the chainsaw; its squeal, its dropping tone when the
engine strained through a stubborn knot.

Sawdust itching the back of our collars, in our hair, under our
eyelids like tiny shards of glass. My eyes streamed from the
toxic two-stroke smoke that blew straight into my face from the
exhaust outlet.

Throwing the hearth sized chunks into the yellow one-tonne
dumper with the crank handle start, puttering up the cowlane
to the big house, trailing a thick plume of diesel smoke into the
damp sky.

I'd handbarrow those logs around the back between the shippen
and the dairy door, through the slurry stench, into the log
bunker. Then back through the cowhouse like Sisyphus.

Oakwood Cemetery on the Sunday
Closest to Your Birthday

The cold rainwater in the leaves
had soaked up my jeans
turning blue to black
and the air was full of rot:
wet wood and bonfire smoke.
Through a cloud of my breath
traffic noise rose from the I-81 as
I reached for the smoothness
of your headstone.

Stormfront

Do you still have the blood dot
on the white of your eye, sister?
A memento of a summer spent
fishing tench (tiny, delicate, silver-green)

out of the flooded quarry.
The bait: a bucket of worms
and broken biscuits.
Keeping score as we stuffed the keepnet.

Our imagined life as survivors, living off
bushmeat and breadfruit,
instead of the thick jam sandwiches
stowed in the tackle box.

The stillness of the water,
the panic of a bite, the returning calm,
the vapour trails from an aeroplane
ploughing the sky, a drift of sleep,

the pineal gland in control, the shape
of a tiny pinecone from an age
when anatomy was figurative.
When the hook caught your eye

from my wayward cast, the silence of shock.
The line sagged between us,
the neon green feather resting on your cheek.
I held my breath to unhook the tear

in your sclera, my fingers foul
with fish innards. Then the roundhousing,
haymaking, great arcing swings of retribution
that junked up my face. When a stormfront
blows through, my jaw still throbs.

Watching the Dog Wake

Every day the same explosive celebration –
with deep gulps her chest fills with the morning,
her tail beats back and forth with such unrestraint
it drags the whole back half of her body with it.
It's as though she can't quite believe her luck
to have been resurrected into flesh, a polished gift.
Yesterday has been forgotten
just as she will have misplaced today by tomorrow.
Bounding to each corner of the kitchen
she sniffs to check on her existence.
This is my favourite part of the day – refilling her bowl,
singing the Golden Girls theme, observing her innocence.
I wonder what she expected. Each night led away
by the wrong brother – Death clutching the scruff of her neck
while Sleep watches on from the riverbank.
If we could talk, I would tell her about my vigil,
seeing her legs twitch, full of phantom running.
I would ask her to describe her meadows, the birdsong.
I would tell her how I called her name in the night
and the gratitude I felt when she chose to return.

Night Whispers

The children are kept hushed,
Any noise louder than the kettle's gentle
rolling boil banned. Quietness
so heavy that it might be death itself
breathing within the darkness. You resolve
the distant from the small;
across town a church bell chimes
with an untethered madness,
blown free of the night, and a coal train
hugs the seam of the Delaware
taking care not to arrive before Trenton.
You long to see that river one last time.
A hiss of unshared whispers surrounds
you like fat spitting from a pan.
A Deathwatch beetle knocks
on a rafter and waits to hear
the mimicked reply of a mate,
a sound once thought to be
the impatient fingers of God.

Argentina

A herd of zebu fatten on the pampas.
A female, the moonlight shifting
across her pendulous dewlap,
keeping time with each chew, swinging
in and out of the cold blue.

A night so clear
the Milky Way is spilt talcum powder,
and this could be any grassland:
the wild-west prairie, an African savanna,
the steppes of Eurasia or back home
in Staffordshire with its familiar moon,

where, as kids, we'd skip stones
at its reflection in the flooded pit
sunk into the heart of the four-acre,
and I'd win; my pockets secretly full
of smashed roof tiles. Their manufactured

flatness equalled perfect skimmers –
ripples upon ripples expanding beyond
the sky's mirrored orbit. The others assumed
my success was down to superior technique –
and in a way, it was.

Dusk

so we choose to remember
some earlier version
when you were ablaze

and caught red-handed
stretched and striving
collecting all you thought

you were owed or further back
before the cognac glow
and the inexplicable temper

before the new claws of winter
began to show themselves
and before the pale creep of dusk

which has always loomed
but now feels bigger
and is getting bigger still

Everyone's a First Generation Something

When I said I was going
to college, they said why,
and well done; bewilderment
coupled with vague celebration.

I hear my home singing,
badly, dropping its aitches;
a piston's high whine
or a conspiracy of airbrakes.

Science states the cello
is closest in tone
to the human voice.
But what does science know?

Waking From the Dream about Ghosts

Full yellow moon, halved to its small blue brother.
The radio's howl rips the lid off the morning.

Stowed sun now untethered. Morning insists
on your attention like a bad storyteller.

A day of memo wars and eating at your desk awaits.
Of getting caught staring at a pretty checkout attendant

and sharply turning away. The brilliant ideas of last night
have slipped into the great coke furnaces of the past,

and the shade of grey you inhabit begins to darken,
while those around you brighten to white.

You are a travelling prizefighter, new to town: unknown
and formidable. All your strengths are your own,

all faults, family heirlooms.

Inheritance

On Calton Hill
looking across the cliffs –
their permanence, their grief –
before they fall into the Forth.
They exist. They might as well
sit within touching distance.
I imagine the ancient heat
trapped within their salts.
I imagine their voices,
deep and slow,
breaking apart, plosive
by thumping plosive.
How I'd love
to announce in a newly cast language
the old language they've lost
in the waves.
Last of my species,
a slab, a tongue of moon.

Potbank

We sort through the seconds,
the spoils, the breakages
from the first biscuit firing.
Tiles still warm from the kiln
like baked potatoes. The dunts
and thermal cracks discarded.
Each tile similar but never
the same, tessellating snugly
yet imperfectly.

The crackle glaze, the crystal
glaze spread over the naked
earthenware, porous surfaces
primed to adhere. Glazed to a mirror
shine, a bright blood moon
and technicolour blues.
Lacquer with the lustre of oil spill.

The permeance of dust
embedded in our hair,
ingrained in our nightly dreams.
Slip and slurry raging through veins
like blood, bones cast from fine bone
china in the city of six towns.

My Father Laid Bricks

My father spent his whole life laying bricks.
One by one, line after line, bedding each
brick down with a few taps of his trowel.
His hands, beaten and coarse, would spread the smooth
mortar like clotted cream along the top
of each full row ready to lay another.
Day and night my father laid the entire
town, working from the slab to the eaves.
He built those walls with an unfamiliar
affection, checking his work was level
And square, plumb and true. He claimed every
street; I cannot walk on a summer's day
without stepping into the shadow of
a building that crushes me with its regret.

Fire, Devour Us

It had been such a splendid afternoon – fishing right off the dock into deep crystal water,
we were Jupiter & Saturn – that I waited until the sky was swollen and cinder orange.
I had a question I'd spent my whole life wording. He was going to be so surprised
when I asked; I doubted he'd ever been loved enough to have been asked before.
He produced a fine bottle of cognac from his knapsack – it must have spent all day
hidden, calling. That's too generous, I said, as he poured two handsome measures.
The first sip brightened by the salt that crusted our lips. I listened carefully
to his preoccupations: declining health, memories of late parents, etc. Tending to his catalogue
of small hurts. Then, when a moment as good as any other arrived, I asked,
what do you think is the purpose of angels? Without turning his gaze from the distance,
he replied, that's not something I want to talk about with you.

Evolving Dusk

And that's how it was:

butter light
                        the late summer, soon to shuffle
            into something
                                    less welcome,

        we held steadfast
                        against this slow death,
                soaking
                                    up the last sun
            like two pieces
of torn bread.

The warmth outmanoeuvred
                    by the dipping horizon.

                            Fireflies ignited
            like small catastrophes,

rising, floating

                                into the half-light,
                                into the semi-dark.

I said dusk,
                    she said twilight.

The Infidelity of Hammocks

Do not allow yourself to be seduced
By hammocks; never fall into their string
Embrace. Those picture postcard scenes produced
For tourists' eyes, in which a local swings
Against the desert sky and coconut
Palms bow down in support of empty lust,
Promise too much. It feels so tempting but
Your bones will bend, unable to adjust.

You will, of course, ignore these words (I did)
Until the hessian claws your shirtless back
And each attempted roll leaves you crooked:
A rabbit, snared, thrashing about for slack.
Then, once the blood has pooled inside your head,
You'll make a graceless dismount for your bed.

I Found Out on Facebook that
My First Girlfriend Had Died

Sadness or at least the sense
of where a sadness might sit
had it not been so long ago.

I'd expected to see her again
in the cereal aisle or collecting a prescription
when home visiting my mum.

Her name is – was – the same as my wife's.
One of those patterns of coincidence you notice
which means absolutely nothing.

I think of her sometimes: long summer
afternoons when her father was at work,
swigging gin from the drinks cabinet,

the novelty of nakedness.
I still have the letters she passed me in class,
in an old biscuit tin somewhere in the loft.

Lockdown (a Love Poem)

The stats show the more hours we spend
in with the ones we choose the more ire
we collect towards them – compelled to inflict
our own presence. Completely dependent
on my love for A and yet I injure her daily
with a thousand small acts of absence.
The more I try to escape myself
I realise how inescapable I am –
dislodging this terrible programming
like trying to detangle a neglected fishing net
that spans the visible distance.

Peafowl

We turn right off the expressway
past Mt. Bonnell and into someone else's heaven:
a small patch of Texas filled with Indian peacocks.
I grew up where the promise of peacocks
unravelled on a school outing
somewhere in Staffordshire; a solitary tattered thing
plucking bare its dulled rainbow of plumage.
But this – this electric muster of birds,
dozens of them roaming the ornamental garden,
crowding the parking lot, calls fat with menace,
voices as malformed as their tails are beautiful.
Two perch upon the roof of the little tearoom.
Another blocks the entrance gate,
its feathers fully fanned like a deck of cards,
a hundred cobalt eyes boring into us.
It steals the sunlight for its own resplendence,
and in the shade left behind
a cluster of plain brown peahens console one another.
We've come here to lift A's spirits;
she's been passed over for a small promotion.
Nothing that will register in a week or two
but today she is stung, and it has left me stung too,
which I think might be a circle closer to love's core.

Stanislavski Method with Coffee

Take the mug's base and slide your fingers
through the handle. Imagine clasping the hilt of a rapier.
Nurse the warmth tentatively, blow cooling ripples
over the surface.

Too much is unknown: fine bone china, coarse
earthenware, or the chipped tin of a prisoner's cup?
The tension of your grip and shape of your palm
a puzzle:

too confident, you fail to embrace the jeopardy of spillage;
too round, you hold a small moon;
too slack, you treasure an illusive, half-remembered dream;
too uneven, you are cradling a dying animal;

too timid and there's nothing in your hand at all.

Galleon

Two voices translated from the debris
of a washed-up galleon

smashed against the laments
of an errant armada.

Two voices: one gruff, a shanty,
bitten by its time at sea,

the other smoothed to glass or polished bronze
where a statue has been touched for luck.

Two voices logged long ago:
one encrusted with wreckage,

the other dug hollow
as if by a melon-baller or ice-cream scoop.

Two voices hacked from the hulls
mid-breath, and transplanted here,

studded with alien textures.
Two fistfuls of ocean still stubbornly

uttering all that they were
and wanted to be.

Voices slipping, fading into quicksand,
slowly eroding under their own surfaces.

Two tightly woven voices: one a wishing-well,
the rattle of change glinting in the deep,

the other salvation or the night,
its stars projected, embedded, a singular moment.

Voices exposed by their skin-picked anxieties,
consumed and reconfigured,

one as blue as Burmese blackwood, the other
more copper than tin, rutilant as tiger's eye.

Zero

You are driving me
to the airport.

How many more times will I see you
in this world?

The answer is scribbled on the back
of an invoice that has fallen

behind the sofa cushions –
a finite number we can't quite calculate.

The radio reports high interest rates & relays
the final scores.

Hungover from your good Scotch.
We have nothing left to say.

I am moving to New York, London,
the Republic of Somewhere Else.

Death guides us by the wrist;
such strong hands.

When the number hits zero
and the call comes to say it's too late,

I'll be distant, unable to search
for the lost scrap of statement.

The radio broadcasting the day's events
with indifference.

Haiku for Refused Hearts

#5

I'm awkward for you.
I'm a hunched weeping willow
With untied laces.

#29

Text message alert,
Running from a cold shower,
It wasn't from him.

#35

I slept with someone
Else to teach you a lesson.
You were out of town.

#41

I call the cat in.
His name leans back in my mouth;
Real as a tattoo.

#44

Lipstick on a glass,
Wooly hat under the bed.
Will you just leave, please?

#50

Christmas Eve party,
Across the room he's laughing.
Why is he laughing?

#67

I hope I'll see her
Crossing a snow laden street
Until I see her.

#82
I think about him
Less and less but never less
Than every moment.

Catch

Our pyro-obsession would lead
us into the thick backwoods

next to the decommissioned railway line,
our pockets stuffed with ribbons

of old newspaper and stolen matches.
When the eyes of the day

had been scooped out, we stacked scraps
of trash and fallen willow sticks

and waited for them to catch.
Huddled around the warmth,

enveloped by oily darkness,
spellbound by our creation.

Curfews came and went
and one-by-one we slipped back

into the ravaged estate.
Just another memory labelled for erasure,

like the ones you can see in my stance
and catch in my voice:

the dark-hearted bark of a rusted exhaust pipe,
an envelope addressed in my father's writing,

an eye tremulous from medication,
the old cinema with smashed-out windows.

Ode to Lake Effect

Your Arctic hands throw glass and shatter
The limbs of oaks in a kind violent manner.

A sugar, a silence, an evidence
Of dog, a cast of gangs, a brilliance

Of hands in bobble hats. Here's the sign
Of a father's slow homecoming

And a fatherless slow oblivion of white
Covers of us, erasures of the beautiful

By the beautiful, versions of water,
Versions of cold folded like A4 card,

Once, twice, four times to prove each one
Of us is a flake and drift and blue.

On Leaving

No sofa to absorb the sound
of my soles striking the parquet floor.
Not a spoon in the drawer.
The cat's paws buttered.
Dishcloth folded.
The final scene surveyed, ticking
off last acts. Meter readings taken.
Key unthreaded from the bunch.
On the counter a note
of encouragement for my next self.

Acknowledgements

Appreciation to the editors of the publications in which some of these poems first appeared: *45th Parallel, Anon, Anthropocene, Bath Magg, Bodega, CURA, Fjords Review, Fourteen, Iron Horse Literary Review, The Interpreter's House, Lascaux Review, The London Magazine, Long Poem Magazine, The Manchester Review, Moon City Review, New Madrid Review, New Ohio Review, The Poetry Review, The Rialto, Switchback.* Some of the poems appeared in the pamphlets: *Lake Effect* (Tapsalteerie Press) and *Trading Zone* (Talbot Rice Gallery).

The writing of these poems was aided by the time and support provided by the following institutions: Arts and Humanities Research Council, Cove Park, Harry Ransom Library – University of Texas at Austin, Isle of Harris Distillers, Moniach Mhor, New York State Summer Writers Institute, Scottish Book Trust, SGSAH (Scottish Graduate School for Arts and Humanities), Society of Authors, Syracuse University, Talbot Rice Gallery.

Heartfelt gratitude to all the friends and mentors who overhauled these poems with me, especially: Adam Bright, Bruce Smith, Brooks Haxton, Dorothy Lawrenson, Grady Chambers, Jane McKie, John Glenday, Lauren Pope, Marianne MacRae, Mary Karr, Michael Burkard, Miriam Gamble, Russell Jones, Sarah Stewart.

Thank you to Rob Mackenzie and Blue Diode Press for believing in this collection.

Tim Craven is from Stoke-on-Trent and lives in Scotland. He has a poetry MFA from Syracuse University and a PhD from the University of Edinburgh, which examined the characterisation of mental illness in Confessional poetry. He received a New Writers Award from the Scottish Book Trust and an Emerging Writer Award from Cove Park. *Good Sons* is his debut collection.

timcraven.co.uk